Mike O'Hara has lived in Wareham for 30 years. His keen interest in local history has led to a long association with Wareham Museum, of which he is currently curator. The recent National Lottery-funded refurbishment of the Museum prompted a review of its photographic collection, which was the inspiration behind this book.

Ben Buxton worked with Mike O'Hara on the redisplay of Wareham Museum. He is a tutor in archaeology in adult education, also a photographer, and he copied most of the photographs in this book. This is his second local history book. He lives in Stoborough.

*Following page*

1. Harvesting oats in the Tyneham valley in 1929.

In this quintessential rural English view, Tyneham is among the trees on the left, and beyond is Worbarrow Bay. Scenes such as this were to come to an abrupt end in December 1943 when the valley and a large area to the east and north were requisitioned by the army for tank training in preparation for the invasion of occupied France, and the population was evacuated. Despite promises that the area would be returned after the war, this never happened, triggering an emotive campaign for the land to be returned to its former owners, or to be placed in the care of a public body such as the National Trust. Neither of these aims was achieved, but the campaign did result in improved public access to the village and the coast path in the 1970s.

# PURBECK CAMERA

MIKE O'HARA AND BEN BUXTON

THE DOVECOTE PRESS

# George H. Cox,

DAY & ARTIFICIAL LIGHT STUDIO,

**No. 5, Institute Road, Swanage,**

**DORSET.**

Dealer in all kinds of CAMERAS, PLATES, FILMS, PAPERS, AND PHOTOGRAPHIC ACCESSORIES.

**DARK ROOM for Amateurs to Change or Develop.**

FILMS AND PLATES developed with great care the same day as received.

2. George Cox's photographic studio in Swanage, 1906.
Many of the photographs in this book were taken by a handful of pioneering Purbeck photographers, without whom books such as this would be virtually impossible. George Cox set up in business in Institute Road in 1904, in competition with Walter Pouncy and Thomas Powell, and retired in 1930. Sadly, very little of his original work survives, as his collection of glass plate negatives was destroyed when Herston House, where he had lived in retirement, was demolished in 1966.

First published in 2001 by The Dovecote Press Ltd
Stanbridge, Wimborne, Dorset BH21 4JD

ISBN 1 874336 90 3



Typeset in Monotype Sabon

Printed and bound in Singapore
A CIP catalogue record for this book is available
from the British Library



1 3 5 7 9 8 6 4 2

# *Contents*

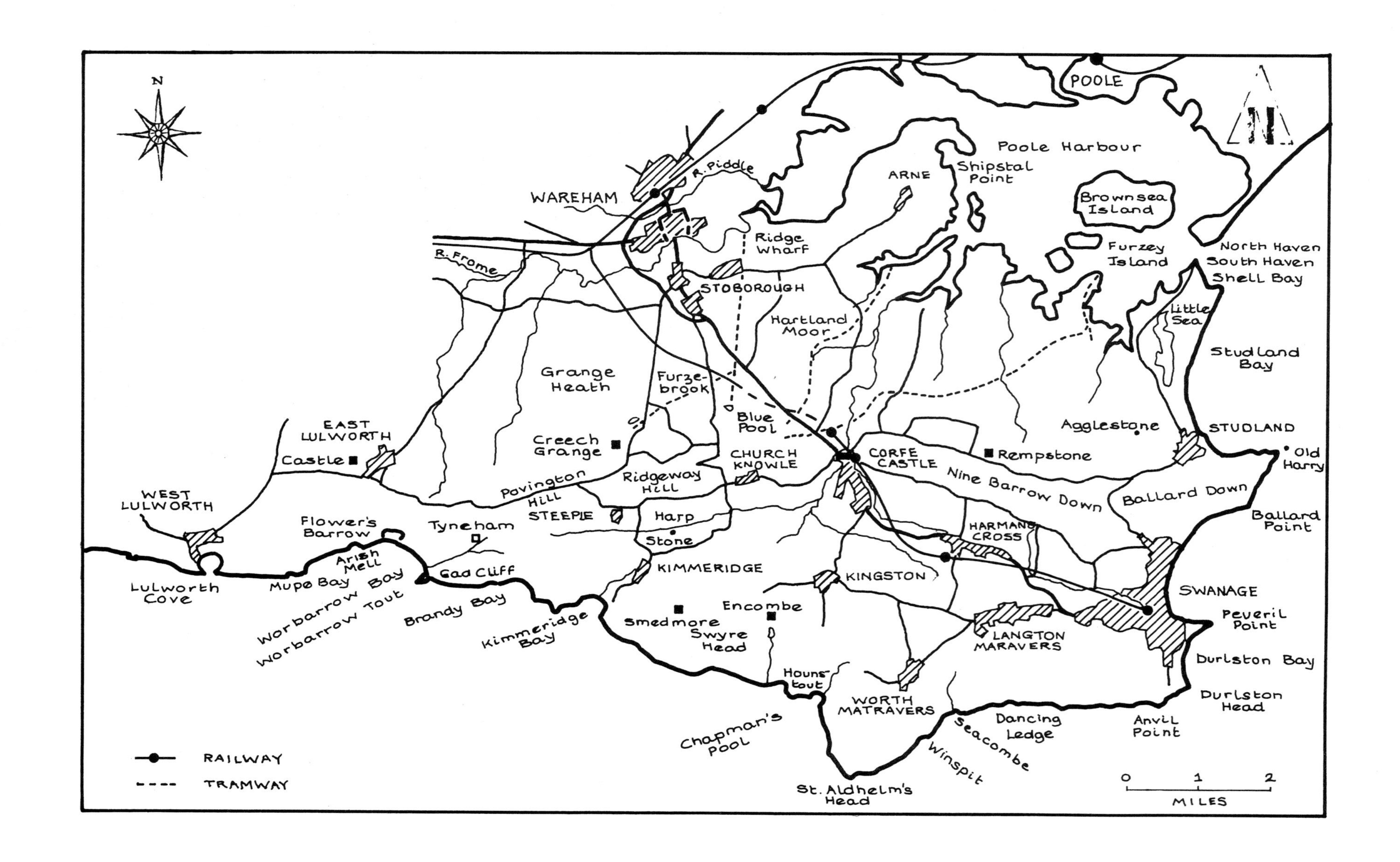
N
POOLE
Poole Harbour
WAREHAM
R. Piddle
ARNE
Shipstal Point
Brownsea Island
Furzey Island
North Haven
South Haven
Shell Bay
Ridge Wharf
R. Frome
STOBOROUGH
Hartland Moor
Little Sea
Studland Bay
Grange Heath
Furze-brook
Blue Pool
Agglestone
STUDLAND
Old Harry
EAST LULWORTH
Castle
Creech Grange
CHURCH KNOWLE
CORFE CASTLE
Rempstone
Nine Barrow Down
Ballard Down
Ballard Point
WEST LULWORTH
Povington Hill
Ridgeway Hill
STEEPLE
Harp Stone
Flower's Barrow
Tyneham
HARMANS CROSS
Arish Mell
Lulworth Cove
Mupe Bay
Gad Cliff
KIMMERIDGE
KINGSTON
SWANAGE
Worbarrow Bay
Worbarrow Tout
Brandy Bay
Kimmeridge Bay
Smedmore
Encombe
Swyre Head
LANGTON MARAVERS
Peveril Point
Durlston Bay
Houns-tout
WORTH MATRAVERS
Durlston Head
Chapman's Pool
Dancing Ledge
Anvil Point
Seacombe
Winspit
St. Aldhelm's Head
RAILWAY
TRAMWAY
0 1 2
MILES

# *Introduction*

For the many thousands who visit south east Dorset for the first time and gaze across the waters of Poole Harbour and Poole Bay, the sight of the distant hills of Purbeck rising up from the sea might convince them that, as its name suggests, this beautiful corner of the county is actually an island. Though not completely surrounded by water, the area's distinctiveness and isolation justifies its historical name, the Isle of Purbeck.

Purbeck was more like an island in the past, when the valley of the River Frome, which forms the western part of its northern boundary, was marshy and often flooded. The western boundary is regarded as being Luckford Lake, an insignificant stream rising east of East Lulworth, and meandering north to the Frome. The Lulworths are thus technically excluded, but they are traditionally considered part of Purbeck. Wareham, although on the north bank of the Frome, is Purbeck's ancient market town and main gateway by land. An early form of the name Purbeck is first recorded in 948 and probably derives from the Old English words for a beak shaped ridge – the chalk ridge – and the bittern or snipe. Most of the village and farm names likewise go back to Saxon times.

The region encompasses within some sixty square miles a great variety of scenery, reflecting the underlying geology. It is dominated by two parallel ridges of hills running east to west for a distance of over twelve miles. The southern ridge, most of it more like a plateau, falls dramatically to the sea in cliffs of limestone, peppered with ancient quarry workings. The northern ridge is a narrow spine composed of chalk. The land between the two ridges is rich and fertile, having been continuously cultivated since prehistoric times. In stark contrast, the land north of the chalk consists mainly of heath, part of Hardy's 'Egdon Heath.' Here the acid soil thinly covers gravels and clays.

Traditionally Purbeck men and women had to turn their hands to anything in order to survive. During the winter months fishermen would become quarrymen, heathland smallholders or 'heath croppers' would dig clay. Even the residents of Wareham were constantly required to diversify in order to make ends meet. It was this ability to exploit the region's natural resources, often in the face of adversity, that has shaped the character of its people.

Throughout history the region's fortunes have been largely determined by demand from outside for its resources or products. Even before the Roman army ordered Purbeck pottery from as far north as Hadrian's Wall, it was in use throughout Iron Age Dorset. The Romans also developed the stone, salt and Kimmeridge shale industries. A thousand years later building stone and decorative stone (the 'Purbeck marble') were again in demand for medieval churches and cathedrals. In the eighteenth century Purbeck became one of the country's major suppliers of clay for the ceramic industry. All these products were exported by sea. The clay and stone industries are still thriving, and in the late twentieth century were joined by another: oil.

In 1847 the Southampton and Dorchester Railway opened, skirting Purbeck's northern borders. Nearly forty years later the branch from Wareham to Swanage reached into the heart of Purbeck. The railways, and the paddle steamers from the 1870s, brought a new phenomenon: tourists. Tourism provided an alternative source of income – selling postcards – for local photographers whose studios were already established to satisfy the Victorian fashion for portraiture. Picture postcards were introduced in

1894 and rapidly became universally popular.

The postcard was a cheap and convenient means of communication. The modern postcard usually depicts a familiar beach or beauty spot, but in the early years, railway stations, gas works, and army camps were all fair game for the postcard trade. Such mundane scenes provide valuable insights into past times. We are also indebted to photographers such as Thomas Powell of Swanage who built his own portable camera using wood from cigar boxes and went out into the streets to record the everyday lives of ordinary people.

This book records aspects of Purbeck life over the past 140 years. It takes the form of a tour, starting at Wareham and proceeding through the heathlands to Studland. We then cross the chalk ridge to Swanage, and head west through coastal communities and inland villages as far as West Lulworth.

## *Acknowledgements*

We would like to thank the following for the use of photographs in their possession or for which they hold the copyright:

Miss J. Barnard: 54; Mr M. Bond: 131, 151, 152; Bournemouth *Daily Echo*: 51, 126, 132, 137, 138, 153 (126, 137, 153 by Arthur Grant); Dr J. Brown: 69; Mr G. Burden: 31, 59; Mrs Burgess: 118, 155, 160; Church Knowle Parochial Church Council: 139-146; Dorset County Museum (special thanks to Miss V. Dicker): 34, 53, 58, 66, 70-73, 75, 76, 78, 79, 81-89, 91-95, 98, 99, 101-109, 111-113, 115, 116, 119, 124, 125, 127, 129, 130, 135, 136, 139, 156, 157, 159; Dovecote Press: 18, 97, 100, 150, 163; ECC Ball Clays Ltd: 55, 56, 60, 63-65; Mrs L. Ladle: 133, 134; Mr J. Patrick: 74, 114, 117, 123, 128; Bob Richardson Photography: 28; Miss L. Seymour: 19, 20; Mrs V. Stevens: 1; Stoborough First School: 11, 41, 43-45, 50, 52, 68; Mrs E. Talbot: 2, 9; The Tank Museum, Bovington: 161; Mrs M. Taylor: 61, 62; Wareham Museum: 3-8, 10, 12-17, 21-27, 29, 30, 32, 33, 35-40, 42, 46-49, 57, 67, 80, 120-122, 158; Mr Andrew Wright, 138.

We are also grateful to the many people who have helped us with information about photographs, especially: Mr H. Bonfield; Mr Bugler; Mr T. Crumpler; Mrs M. Duncan; Mr J. Ford; Mr P. Gould; the late Mr G. Gover; Mr A. Hancock; Mr A. Hill; Mr T. Salter; Mrs D. and Mr V. Savage; Mr R. Saville; Mr D. Smale; Mr W. Smith; Mrs Stockley.

# *Wareham*

3. The level crossing at Northport, Wareham, about 1910. For nearly 150 years this was the main 'gateway' to Purbeck by land, and most traffic bound for Purbeck had to negotiate it. In this south-facing view the name of Groves, the Weymouth brewery, can be seen on the gable of the Railway Hotel. The two buildings on the right were crossing keepers' cottages. The crossing was a bottleneck for traffic for many years before it closed in 1980 on completion of the northern section of the Wareham bypass.

4. Wareham's first railway station, about 1870. This was the original Southampton and Dorchester Railway station, opened in 1847. It was sited to the east of the level crossing, which is just visible at the far end of the platforms. The building continued in use as staff accommodation into the 1970s, when it was demolished. The original goods shed, off the left edge of this view, still stands.

5. A carriage at the entrance to Wareham's second station, 1890s. On 16th May 1885 the branch line from Wareham to Swanage opened to traffic. The old station site was too cramped to accommodate the extra line and platform, so a new station, the present one, was built west of the level crossing in 1886.

6. Wareham Station 'down' platform, early 1900s. This train, worked by an Adams tank locomotive, is probably a through stopping service from Bournemouth to Swanage. In 1900 the 134 mile journey by express from Swanage to London took just over three hours, and a return third class ticket cost 22 shillings (£1.10). On the right of the picture, looking east, is the buffer stop of the Swanage Branch bay. The branch line closed in 1972 and this area is now used for car parking.

7. Wareham Gas Works, North Street, 1938. A gas works was established on the south east side of North Bridge in 1840, making town gas from coal to light the streets, some public buildings, and later, houses. The two engines that drove the generators of the Bournemouth Electric Company's plant at West Walls at the end of the century were also powered by town gas. The gas works are pictured here just before they were demolished and rebuilt by the Bournemouth Gas and Water Company, which built the show room that still stands on North Street, and new gas cylinders. The works closed in the early 1970s when North Sea gas came on stream.

8. North Mill and North Walls, about 1910. A mill on this site was first mentioned in the 12th century. The mill ceased to operate at the end of the 19th century, since when it has been a house. On the right is the northern section of the Saxon town walls, which surround Wareham on three sides. Just visible in the distance are North Bridge and the chimneys of the gas works.

9. St Martin's Church, North Street, 1920s. The church is the most complete late Saxon church in Dorset. It was subsequently enlarged and modified but became disused during the 18th century. It was used to shelter people made homeless by the great fire of 1762. The church contains an effigy of T.E. Lawrence ('Lawrence of Arabia'). Just visible at the bottom of the hill is the sign of the Lord Nelson, which closed in 1982, and the buildings of the gas works.

10. North Street, looking south, about 1880. Various signs adorn the buildings on the left, including those of the Greyhound Inn (which closed in about 1885) and James Bridle, photographer, who probably took this view. On the near corner of Cow Lane, on the right, is the medieval Allhallow's Chapel, by this time a barn, which was demolished in the late 1880s. The stone-lined gutters were flushed daily, a necessary task when livestock were tethered overnight in town and the use of horse power was universal.

11. (*Above*) Postmen outside Wareham Post Office, about 1912. The postal district of Wareham extended far beyond the confines of the town, and with four daily deliveries and a telegram service to maintain, a large staff was necessary. The office was open to the public from 8am to 9pm Monday to Saturday, 8 to 10am Sunday. The post office moved to its present site further up the street in the 1930s, and the old building became the Labour Exchange, later the Job Centre. Left to right: George Selby, William Randall (telegram deliverer), Eddie Crumpler, all of Stoborough; Herbie Crombes; unknown; Mr Baberstock; unknown; Mr Brown; Harry Selby of Stoborough; unknown.

12. (*Above right*) Percy Tewkesbury. The 1907 camp for boys held on Brownsea Island by Lord Baden Powell marked the birth of the Scouting Movement, and the Wareham pack was one of the earliest to be formed, probably in 1908 when this photograph was taken.

13. A telegraph pole on the move in North Street, 1900s.

14. A cavalry or mounted infantry regiment in North Street, about 1898. Soldiers were a common sight in Wareham around the time of the Boer War. Large areas on the outskirts of the town were used as training grounds for soldiers prior to posting to South Africa. 'Buller's Army', under the leadership of General Buller, set up camp on Trigon Heath in 1898. Local photographer William Churchill received written permission from Buller himself to photograph troop manoeuvres, and this photograph was probably taken by him.

15. Frisby's shoe shop, North Street, about 1930. The shop was then managed by Mr Lionel Guppy (centre) who later established his own shop on the other side of the street. Guppy's is still trading in 2001.

16. The Town Hall, about 1860. This Town Hall was built shortly after the fire of 1762, which destroyed much of Wareham. It was built on the site of the medieval church of St Peter, which had been used as a civic building for over a century. John Calcraft, Lord of the Manor and local MP, was active in promoting the town's regeneration. The building was replaced by the present Town Hall in 1870. The boys in this early photograph are obligingly keeping very still for the long exposure.

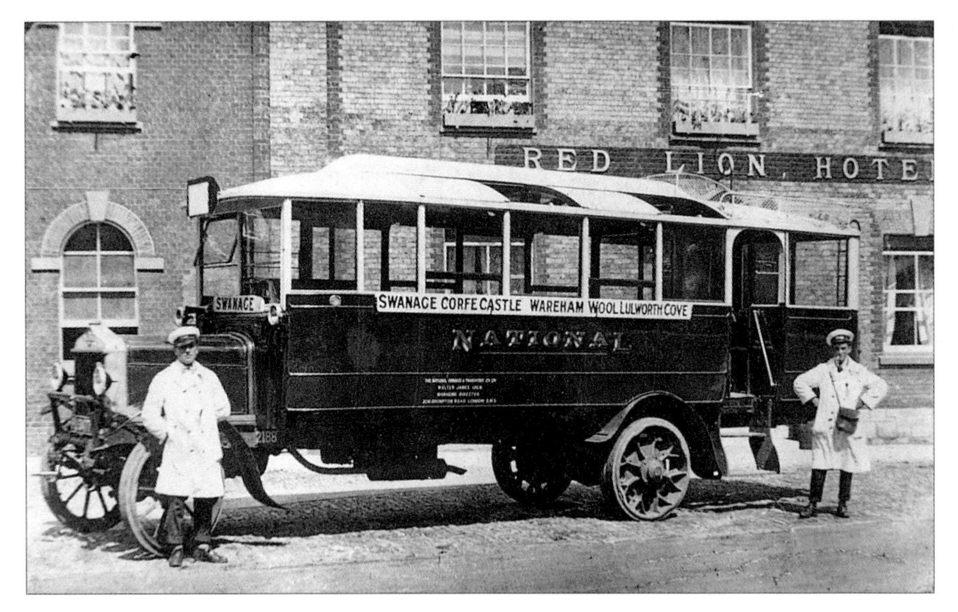


17. A National bus outside the Red Lion Hotel, North Street, 1920s. By the mid 1920s the bus had begun to challenge the monopoly on rural transport previously held by the railways. Vehicles like this A.E.C. 'Y' type were instrumental in the growth of the tourist industry in the region. A journey around Purbeck's untarred roads must have been slow and uncomfortable, especially on solid tyres.

18. West Street, late 1950s. This view, looking towards the Cross (the central cross roads), shows how the motor car was beginning to dominate the streets. The building with the Esso sign is Cleeve's Garage which started life in the 1890s as a wheelwright and cycle repairer. The petrol storage tanks were buried beneath the sitting room which was heated by a coal fire! The garage ceased trading in the 1970s and the building became a pet shop.

19. Arthur Wade hand milking at Worgret Farm in the 1940s before he set up his own business. Hand milking died out in the 1950s when the introduction of milking machines revolutionised the dairy industry.

20. Wareham Dairy. Arthur Wade started a milk delivery business in West Street in the late 1940s. He was a well known figure in the town, being choirmaster and organist at Lady St Mary's Church. Delivery boy Ken Wellstead is seated on the D.O.T. motorcycle alongside the Ford 8 van.

21, 22. Two views of Wareham's Spring ('Cuckoo') Fair, April 1912. Agricultural fairs had been held in Wareham, Purbeck's market town, since ancient times and the top view from West Walls shows the livestock sale. This site is now a car park, and the open land beyond is occupied by the houses of Monmouth Road. In the distance in the top photograph is the former workhouse, built in 1837. This has now been converted into housing association accommodation and is known as Christmas Close. In addition to the Spring Fair there was a Michaelmas Fair in September. There were also weekly markets held at the Cross and later in East Street, and 'Jeff's market' on a site now known as Coopers Close in Mill Lane.

23. George Dicker, late 1930s. Mr Dicker established his grocery business in West Street in the late 1870s, and he later opened another shop on the corner of West Street and South Street. He is best remembered for the legendary 'Dicker's Dorset Sausages,' whose recipe George kept secret and alas, took with him to the grave. George served on the town council and was mayor from 1906 to 1908. This picture was originally a commemorative card, in whose margin someone has scribbled the cost of chair covers.

24. East Street, Wareham, about 1860. This view, looking towards the Cross and the old Town Hall, shows the bustle of an election day. Street photographs of this period are rare, and this picture aptly conveys the atmosphere of Anglebury, Hardy's name for Wareham. In the left foreground is one of the town pumps. By the end of the century, contaminated drinking water was a serious public health hazard, and in 1906 a clean supply was piped in from Worgret.

25. Charles Major, about 1960. Mr Major was a master shoemaker who moved to Wareham from Cerne Abbas, where he served his apprenticeship, in the early 1900s. He set up as a cobbler in Trinity Lane, and later moved to East Street. In his later years he made shoes for Guppy's. He finally retired in the early 1960s at the age of 82.

26. An army aeroplane at North Bestwall Farm, August 1912. This biplane landed at Bestwall, at the invitation of the mayor, during exercises of the Territorials in Purbeck. Here the pilot, Major Webb of the Royal Flying Corps (forerunner of the RAF), explains the mysteries of powered flight to a fascinated crowd. The barn is now a house.

27. South Street, Wareham, looking north, about 1920. On the left, on the corner of Trinity Lane, is Northover's Model Bakery. Beyond is Riggs Brothers greengrocer's, and the white sign is an early branch of Frisby's shoe shop. The silhouette of the black bear, centre, adorns the hotel's elegant porch. Hotel patrons could alight from the London coach in shelter while staff on top of the porch unloaded their luggage from the coach roof. The boys are thought to be members of the Newbery family who lived in one of the cottages on the right. The cottages were demolished to widen the road after the new South Bridge opened in 1927.

28. An 'incident' in South Street, 1988. On an April evening a policeman attempted to arrest a local youth in South Street, and within minutes crowds of Saturday night drinkers were on the streets. Police reinforcements arrived and the whole event turned into a minor 'riot.' Several of the 27 police cars attending were damaged and one was nearly overturned. The 1980s saw a number of well publicised 'public disorder events' in big cities, but these incidents also occurred in rural towns, albeit on a smaller scale.

SMITHS
ENGINEERS

WM. POND. LTD

31. (*Above*) William Burden of Steeple at the wheel of Dr Kilcoursie Courtenay's motor car (a Panard) in Pound Lane in the 1900s. Mr Burden had previously been chauffeur for the Bonds of Creech Grange. These early vehicles were somewhat unreliable and drivers had to double as mechanics. Dr Courtenay, the town's medical officer, was instrumental in securing a safe water supply for Wareham, from Worgret. He was horrified by the state of the supply in the 1890s, which then came from wells contaminated by sewage from cesspits and drains.

29. (*Opposite page top*) The Barn, St John's Hill, about 1930. Newbery and Sons began trading in the 1870s as blacksmiths and wagon builders, and by 1920 they had several workshops in the area. The metal working was carried out in the 15th century barn in St John's Hill, the oldest secular building in Wareham. The wagons and carriages were built in a workshop in Howard's Lane. Newbery's also built batches of wagons for Pike Brothers' narrow gauge clay railway.

30. (*Opposite page bottom*) Bill Pond in the doorway of his shop, mid 1960s. Mr Pond took over Newberys' premises in the 1940s and set up as an agricultural merchants. The shop was a former smithy. This area of St John's Hill was known as Sawpits because, as late as the 1920s, baulks of timber were hand sawn across two long pits. Ponds is one of Wareham's longest surviving businesses.

32. Henry Thorne and 'Jimmy' Habgood with specimen salmon at the Quay, late 1930s. Thorne and Habgood were both river men who spent their lives fishing and wildfowling. The tradition of salmon netting in the estuary of the River Frome goes back to medieval times. Until the 1960s the Lord of the Manor controlled the fishing rights of both rivers and certain estate tenants rented properties which had fishing rights attached to them.

33. Bridge building at the Quay, 1915. As part of their training while based at Wareham Camp the Royal Engineers were required to build a footbridge across the River Frome at the Quay. In the background is the old South Bridge which was replaced by the current concrete one in 1927. In the distance the chimneys of Panton's Brewery and Bennett's Brewery, and Holy Trinity Church can be seen.

34. Building the new South Bridge, 1926. Wareham's traffic problems began as early as the 1920's when the old single carriageway bridge became a bottleneck for the increasing motor traffic. Here we see the east side of the new bridge being constructed alongside the old one, which was originally Norman but rebuilt in 1778. When this side was completed, the old bridge was demolished and the west side of the new bridge was built. During the demolition, the Norman foundations were revealed. Some of the stonework was built into the new Trigon House, north west of Wareham. Work on the new bridge suffered a setback when the jib of the contractor's crane – which ran on the rails on the temporary bridge – broke. It was mended by James Crumpler of Stoborough.

STRONG'S ROMSEY ALES

36. (*Above*) Beating of the Bounds, Wareham Quay, late 1950s. The ancient custom of beating the 'Admiralty Jurisdiction water bounds' between Wareham and Poole required the mayor of Wareham, in this case Harry Broughton (seen here to the right of the priest, addressing the crowd) to inspect the boundary markers. Sandwiched between two ex-landing craft is the most distinguished of Poole's lifeboats, the *Thomas Kirk Wright,* a veteran of Dunkirk, where she ferried troops from the beaches to waiting warships.

35. (*Opposite page*) The Town Quay, early 1900s. This picturesque part of the town was a commercial port and the basis of Wareham's wealth in medieval times, but by the 14th century the river was silting up and Poole was taking over as a port. By the time this picture was taken the only goods landed here were grain for the town's two breweries and coal. The horse-drawn water bowser was provided by the borough council for street cleaning duties, and during the summer the gravel road surfaces were sprayed with water to keep the dust down. On the right is the Rising Sun Inn, which closed in 1931. In the background is Lady St Mary's Church, founded in the eighth century and substantially rebuilt in 1840.

37. Army camp on Worgret Road, 1914. Wareham has a long tradition of hosting summer camps for regimental training. Following the outbreak of the First World War, the town became a mustering point for territorial reservists and volunteers. The first contingent arrived to an unprepared camp and had to be accommodated by townspeople. In this view, on what is now the recreation ground, the camp is being set up, aided by barrels of Bitter Ale. West Walls and the houses of Worgret Road are seen in the background.

38. Surplus bread, 1914. Northover's Bakery had the contract to supply Wareham Camp with bread. In August 1914 a party of 500 soldiers arrived at the camp, hurriedly leaving a few days later following the declaration of war. Mr Northover was left with 1000 loaves, which he distributed free to the townspeople.

39. An army field bakery, Wareham Camp, 1915. Wood fires were lit in these turf-insulated ovens, allowed to die down, and then the bread was baked over the embers.

40. Wareham Camp, Worgret Road, 1916. In 1915 tents gave way to a permanent camp of wooden huts, spread out on either side of Worgret Road. By 1917 the camp held around 7,000 men, and had its own cinema, hospital and sewage works. It also had its own railway siding with loading bays for tanks, then a newly-invented secret weapon. This view, looking east from Worgret, shows part of the camp on the north side of Worgret Road, with the railway cutting in the foreground and the workhouse on the left. Arne Hill is in the distance.

# *Stoborough*

41. A car braving a flooded South Causeway, about 1920. Before the height of the south bank of the river was raised, the meadows, known as East Tidemoor and West Tidemoor, were prone to regular flooding. In earlier times flat bottomed boats were used for the crossing when the meadows were flooded.

42. The South Causeway blocked by snow, February 1977. After a heavy blizzard Wareham found itself completely cut off and essential supplies were delivered by the army using tracked vehicles.

43. A new village hall arrives in Stoborough, about 1920. A section of hut from the former army camp at Worgret is on its way to a new life as a village hall for Stoborough. It stood on the green until 1956 when the present hall was built. On the far right is Bill Randall of Stoborough Farm, next to him William Marsh of Ridge Farm, front left Harry Allen, who was shipwright at Ridge Wharf for Pike Brothers, the clay company. The cart was a timber cart on loan from Pike Brothers, and the horses were William Marsh's.

44. Corfe Road, Stoborough, about 1910. The white building with the bow window at the top of the rise, centre, was Horace Head's grocery and the post office. The gap in the centre right was later partly filled by Gay's Stores, the site of the present village shop and post office.

45. Stoborough garage, mid 1920s. The garage was established in 1918, either by James Crumpler of Stoborough, or by John Thomas Cleeve who was proprietor by 1920. The family of Reginald Churchill, owner at the time this photograph was taken, had a garage in East Street, Wareham. The bus is a Crossley. The cottages were demolished in the 1930s to make way for a much bigger garage.

# *Ridge*

46. Ridge Wharf, 1911. Ridge Wharf, on the River Frome, was the terminus of Pike Brothers' narrow gauge railway, built in 1840 for transporting clay from the pits at Furzebrook and Grange. The shallow-draught sailing vessels seen in this view, looking south, were loaded with clay bound for London. The steam tug was used for pulling barges full of clay to Poole Quay for transhipment to deeper-draught vessels for export to other ports and overseas. Clay export continued up to the Second World War, when the Admiralty took over the wharf for repairing landing craft, and the heath crossed by the railway was taken over by the army for training purposes. The wharf is now a boatyard.

47. Loading clay at Ridge Wharf, 1920s. Here we see a railway wagon tipping its load into a barge. The wagons originally trundled down the line by gravity. On one occasion the system for stopping them at the wharf failed and five loaded wagons careered off the end, sinking the barge below.

48. A clay train on its way to Ridge Wharf, 1911. In 1866 steam power was introduced on the line, and here we see the locomotive *Tertius*, built by Manning and Wardle in 1886.

49. Thomas Powell's cement works at Ridge, 1900. At the time this photograph was taken Ridge was a hive of industrial activity, with the railway and wharf, as well as the cement works. The works opened in 1875, and used chalk and marl from quarries at Cocknowle, south of East Creech. The chalk was hauled to Ridge by cart, and was baked in the kilns seen in the picture. Cement and agricultural lime were produced. The works closed in about 1910, and the buildings were demolished some years later. The site is now occupied by Old Kiln Road and part of Barndale Drive.

# *Arne*

50. Shipstal Point, Arne, and Poole Harbour, 1930s. This scene is barely recognisable today as the cottages were destroyed in the Second World War, and trees have grown up in the foreground. This area is now a RSPB reserve and a haven of tranquillity, but during the war it was heavily bombed. The Royal Naval Cordite Factory at nearby Holton Heath was a prime target for German bombers, so a decoy was set up near Bank Gate Cottages. A mock building was set ablaze with paraffin when a raid was expected, luring the bombers. This successfully saved the factory but over 200 bombs fell on the Arne peninsula.

51. Arne village in ruins, 1950: taken from a contemporary newspaper. These buildings were damaged by a German raid on 3rd June 1942, and suffered further when the Arne peninsula was taken over by the army shortly afterwards, for training troops for the invasion of occupied France. Like the much better known case of Tyneham, the inhabitants were evacuated, but unlike Tyneham, they were allowed back. Few returned. The schoolhouse, on the right, was built in 1874 and closed in 1922. It became a house and was eventually renovated, but the farmhouse of Arne Farm, on the left, had to be demolished. A new house was built which was itself later replaced by the present house.

# *Holme Lane*

52. The toll house, Holme Lane, 1920s. Holme Lane is a quiet leafy by-way, but before the late 18th century it was the main road connecting Wareham with Wool and the west. The construction of the turnpike road through Worgret and East Stoke to Wool, the present main road, made it somewhat redundant. The toll house, known as Toll Bar Cottage, stood on the corner of Holme Lane and Grange Road. It was deemed unfit for human habitation and demolished in 1958. The sign on the left prohibited large vehicles from using the lane.

53. Crossing the ford in Holme Lane, 1905. One of the characteristics of Holme Lane and the hamlet of East Holme was crossing the fords. The stream crossing Holme Lane was eventually bridged but the ford continued in use for car washing. This picture captures the charm of early motoring on empty Edwardian roads. The car is an Adams Hewitt.

# *Furzebrook*

54. Blue Pool, Furzebrook, late 1930s. This popular beauty spot was once a huge clay pit, dug in the 1840s. The clay, found on the heathland of northern Purbeck, has been used for pottery making since prehistoric times. Today's clay industry dates from the 17th and 18th centuries, when demand for clay tobacco pipes, tea cups and teapots was booming. Wedgewoods used Purbeck clay. The Blue Pool opened as an attraction, complete with the tearoom seen here, in 1935, since when the small trees in the picture have matured. The water can appear blue due to the effect of clay particles in suspension in the water.

55. Clay cutters in a clay pit, 1960s. Clay extraction was once a highly labour-intensive industry. Teams of men standing on narrow terraces cut the clay from the face using spades called *tubals*, which may be the origin of the term 'ball clay'. The wagons ran on a network of narrow gauge railways which conveyed the clay to weathering beds and then to quays on the River Frome and Poole Harbour, and to the main line at Furzebrook. The railways closed in 1956/7 and transport is now by road. Jammy Marshallsay (left) and Gilbert Smith are seen here using pneumatic spades and filling the dragline bucket between them. All hand digging in pits was replaced by mechanical excavator in the 1970s.

56. Jack Abbott mining clay, about 1970. The best clay is found deep underground, and during the 20th century dozens of mines were sunk to extract it. It was dug by hand, in later years using pneumatic spades, and brought to the surface on wagons, either cable-hauled if the shaft was inclined, or by a lift arrangement. Jack Abbott worked at Squirrel Cottage mine, Holme Lane. The last mine closed in 1999 and there are currently six open pits, operated by ECC Ball Clays Ltd which bought out the amalgamated Pike and Fayle operations in 1969. The clay is used for fine ceramics and tiles, much of it overseas.

57. Mr Fry, an old clay worker, arriving at work by donkey, 1911. Mr Fry was known as 'the donkey man' as he was in charge of workers' donkeys. If Mr Fry was about to go down a mine, he would have had to leave his pipe behind as naked flames were prohibited underground: pockets of inflammable gas were encountered and rotting pit props gave off gas. Snuff was a popular alternative.

# *Creech*

58. The beagle pack, Creech Grange, about 1890. Beagles were first kept at Creech by the Bond family in the 1850s, but the pack shown here was short-lived, due to a conflict of interest with the shooting tenants.

59. Grange cricket team, Creech, 1922. Cricket was played at Creech before the First World War. After the war it was revived by Ted Burden, seated at bottom right. Mr Burden was a local postman and such was his enthusiasm that after a 4am start on his round he would return to Creech, cut and roll the pitch and participate in the game. Other team members were employed at the 'big house' (Creech Grange), such as 'Father' Beauchamp, the head gardener, far left. On the far right is Bobby Samways. Cricket is still played at Creech today.

# West Creech

60. (*Above*) West Creech clay mine, about 1950. This mine was situated west of West Creech Farm and was served by a branch of the narrow gauge railway from Furzebrook. It was the most westerly of the Pike Brothers' mines. The shaft was vertical, and a double cage arrangement (centre) allowed wagons full of clay to come up at the same time as empties going down. The shed for the winding mechanism is on the right. On the left is the shed where wagons from underground unloaded clay into surface wagons. The mine closed when most of the Pike and Fayle railway network was abandoned in 1956/7.

61. (*Opposite page top*) Orchard Cottages, West Creech, about 1915. Bert, Percy and Elsie Taylor, of nearby Rookery Farm, are seen here with their aunt Beatrice Charles (right) outside her home. The cottages lay inside the area, including Tyneham, which was taken over by the army in 1943, and are now in ruins.

62. (*Opposite page bottom*) Mabel Cake (later Taylor) milking at West Creech Farm, 1926. The farm was a dairy farm, and the left-hand ground floor room of the farmhouse was the dairy, the room above, the cheese loft. The last tenant was Reginald Cake and his family. The farm was also requisitioned by the army in 1943. The Cake family had a month's notice to quit, and received no compensation. The farmhouse is now derelict, but some of the farm buildings are still used by the tenant farmer who grazes cattle on the land. A good deal of the former farmland has been consumed by the huge Povington clay pit, which has encroached to within a few yards of the farmhouse.

# East Creech

63. (*Above*) Cottage at East Creech, about 1900. This 17th century thatched cottage once served as the village bakery. Thatch was the traditional roofing method in northern Purbeck, while stone slates were more common south of the ridge where suitable stone was plentiful. This scene has hardly changed over the past century.

64. (*Opposite page top*) Cotness clay pit and mine, East Creech, about 1950. Cotness was unusual in that it had a mine at the bottom of the open pit. The mine, with a 120 feet deep vertical shaft, was sunk in about 1920 and closed in 1954. Here the locomotive *Sextus* is pulling wagons loaded with clay from the mine. *Sextus* was a saddle tank built by Pecketts in 1925. The six coupled wheel arrangement caused problems on the sharp curves so it was altered on the suggestion of the driver, Mr Gover. On the far right the neat hand-cut faces and delivery chutes to the wagons can be seen.

65. (*Opposite page bottom*) Clay mine at East Creech, about 1950. This extraordinary structure was on the east flank of Creech Barrow near the road from East Creech to Cotness. Wagons loaded with clay from the mine (thought to have been called 'The Common') were attached to a continuous cable, driven by a winch housed in the shed at the top of the staging. The side-tipping wagons unloaded the clay into wagons running on the track underneath. The summit of Creech Barrow is off the picture to the right; Keeper's Cottage can just be glimpsed on the left.

# *Norden*

66. Furze gatherers west of Norden Farm, 1899. Apart from clay, the heath was unproductive, and its inhabitants were amongst the poorest in Purbeck. They eked out a living by gathering furze (gorse) for lighting fuel, particularly for bread ovens. It was also used for packing material by pottery manufacturers at Sandford, north of Wareham. The furze gatherers were known as 'furze hackers' (pronounced 'vurzackers' locally). Corfe Gap can be seen in the distance.

67. Fayle's Middlebere railway, Norden, 1890s. In 1806 Benjamin Fayle, a London potter, commissioned a railway for transporting clay from pits at Norden, north of Corfe Castle, to Middlebere Quay, on an inlet of Poole Harbour. It was Dorset's first railway, technically a plateway, having L-section rails (plates) on stone sleepers, and the trucks had flangeless wheels. Here horses pull a line of five 2-ton wagons in the direction of Middlebere, past houses which still stand near New Line Farm.

68. Fayle's works at Norden, 1890s. This picture, taken a short distance west of the previous one, shows Fayle's offices and smithy (right). The original line crosses from left to right; the two loops were laid after the Swanage branch of the main line was built in 1885. Fayle's line was abandoned in 1905 when the company opened a new line from Norden to Newton. This joined an existing line, worked by steam locomotives, from pits at Newton to a deep-water quay on the Goathorn peninsula. This line in turn closed in 1939 but short lengths of track remained in use at Norden until 1970. This area is now wooded, with only one bungalow on the site. Arne Hill is in the far distance.

69. The old isolation hospital, between Wareham and Corfe Castle, 1967. This was one of many isolation hospitals built throughout the country in 1902 following a major outbreak of smallpox. It stood on the heath not far from the Halfway Inn, and was built of galvanised iron. Although a smallpox case was never admitted, it did treat cases of other infectious diseases. It closed in 1960 and today both it and the adjoining caretaker's/nurse's quarters are let as holiday accommodation by the National Trust.

70. Arfleet Mill, Norden, about 1900. The mill was on the Corfe River half a mile north of Corfe Castle, and was known as Steam Flour Mills in the later 19th century. All these buildings were destroyed by Fayle's clay workings in the 1920s, and the area is now a confusion of overgrown old workings and railway lines. The picture was taken from East Hill.

# *Studland*

71. The Agglestone, Studland Heath, about 1910. This block of iron-rich sandstone, or 'heathstone,' situated amidst desolate heathland overlooking Studland Bay and Poole Harbour, tilted abruptly to the right (south) in 1970. It was called the Devil's Night Cap locally, and according to legend, the devil threw it at Corfe Castle from the Isle of Wight, out of jealousy at the building of the castle: he missed.

72. (*Above*) Studland Village, about 1900. All that survives of the cart shed on the left is the right hand stone wall. On the mound on the right a medieval stone cross base can be seen. This remained vacant for centuries until 1976 when a new cross, carved by Treleven Haysom and featuring designs ancient and modern was put up. The notice on the tree reads 'ANY PERSONS STEALING FERNS, SAND, EARTH OR PEAT WILL BE PROSECUTED WITHOUT FURTHER NOTICE. BY ORDER.' (of the Bankes Estate). This area was the centre of the village before its Edwardian red brick expansion, and the village stocks stood nearby until 1850. The cottages in the background have gone.

73. (*Opposite page*) Sheep shearing at Studland Manor Farm, about 1900.

74. The Bankes Arms, Studland, about 1910. This hotel, near the National Trust car park and the footpath to South Beach, remains much the same. The inn's most famous landlord was Sergeant William Lawrence, whose military career is recorded on his gravestone in the churchyard, and the more colourful details of his life in an autobiography. He was a veteran of the Napoleonic Wars and Waterloo, returning to his native Studland with a French wife. On retirement from the Duke of Wellington, as it then was, he lived in the cottage on the left, long since demolished.

75. Beach Road, Studland, 1890s. Vine Cottage, behind the trap, still stands.

76. Beach huts and cafe at 'Middle Beach', Studland, about 1915.

77. A demonstration of inshore oil defences in Studland Bay, 1940. This particular anti-invasion demonstration was not a success as the wind changed, setting the cliffs alight, and forcing the senior officers viewing it to beat a hasty retreat. Like Arne, the Studland peninsula and a large area to the west were taken over by the army during the war, for training for the invasion of occupied France. At Redend Point near Studland is Fort Henry, a huge concrete observation bunker used by Churchill, Montgomery and Eisenhower for watching the practice invasion exercises of 1943-44.

78. (*Above*) Old Harry Rocks, about 1890. Old Harry is named after Harry Pye, a Poole pirate who, according to legend, lurked here preying on ships; alternatively, the name could refer to the devil. Old Harry is seen in the centre of this view from the north west. He is accompanied by his wife, on the left, but he now stands alone, for his wife succumbed to a storm in 1896. These chalk cliffs and stacks at the easternmost extremity of Purbeck are eroding comparatively quickly: until the 17th century 'Studland Castle' stood somewhere here, also a 'block-house', probably dating to the reign of Henry VIII.

79. (*Above right*) A short distance south of Old Harry is Parson's Barn, a great cavern in the cliff with a beach inside it, once used for landing and storing contraband; the roof collapsed in 1963.

80. South Haven and Poole Harbour, 1929. Before the chain ferry across the mouth of Poole Harbour between South Haven and Sandbanks was introduced in 1926, various piers were in use on the harbour shore of the Studland peninsula. This stone pier, already long disused in this picture, served the inn which stood on the site of the present restaurant until the early 20th century. Beyond is wooded Brownsea Island, part of Studland parish.

# *Swanage*

81. Swanage Bay from the slopes of Ballard Down, 1898. Until the late 19th century, Swanage was hardly more than a village in the south west corner of the bay. In this view, the growth of 'New Swanage' has begun to the north, streets are being laid out and the Grand Hotel, centre left, is nearing completion. Much of the intervening land up to Whitecliff Farm in the bottom left corner has since been built up.

82. The 'stone bankers,' about 1875. For over three hundred years until the end of the 19th century Swanage served as a port for the export of building stone and decorative 'marble' from the nearby quarries. Here stone can be seen awaiting loading into high-wheeled carts which were driven into the sea and unloaded into small boats. These in turn unloaded into larger vessels. This method continued even after a pier, and a tramway leading to it, were built in 1860. This area is now occupied by The Parade and Institute Road. The large building left of centre is the Mowlem Institute, which was replaced by the Mowlem Theatre in 1965.

83. The junction of Shore Road and Victoria Avenue, about 1890. The growing popularity of sea bathing during Victorian times helped the town's development as a resort. The bathing machines were dragged into the sea, allowing bathers to change into their swimming attire and enter the water without shocking anybody. There were separate bathing areas for men and women, and machine proprietors who allowed mixed bathing in these areas could be fined.

84. Swanage from Peveril Point, about 1900. The monument was originally erected in London as a memorial to the Duke of Wellington. In 1867 it was dismantled by George Burt, partner in the building firm set up by his uncle John Mowlem, and he brought it to his home town.The smaller of the two piers was built in 1860 for the export of stone. The larger, 'new' pier, was built adjacent to it in 1896 for the use of paddle steamers from Bournemouth and Poole. The steamer service was introduced in 1874 and finally ceased in 1966. The new pier subsequently deteriorated but has since been restored to its former glory.

85. Ploughing above Shore Road, about 1895.

86. Loading stone from a horse-drawn wagon on the old pier into a sailing ship, about 1890. Such scenes were rare, as the stone merchants preferred the old method of shipping stone out to barges using high-wheeled carts to paying the pier's tolls. The original plan was for the tramway to connect to the stone quarries and also to the projected branch of the main line from Wareham; neither of these happened, although a siding was built to the bankers from the main line after it arrived in 1885. After the opening of the new pier, the old pier was used for coaling the steamers. It went out of use around 1914 and only stumps remain.

87. The tramway and pier approach, about 1895. The tollhouse where the merchants paid for the use of the pier is on the right. In the centre is Walter Prouten, a former coastguard who was reputed to have caught the 'last' smuggler. On the left is a Miss Burt. The tramway was originally laid to standard gauge but it was converted to narrow gauge in 1896.

88. A group on the shore, 1895. Walter Prouten, right, stands next to Phineas Harden, well known for his use of strong language. On the left is James Haysom. This photograph, like others reproduced here, was taken by local photographer Thomas Powell, who, unusually for the period, captured the everyday lives of local people.

89. Tom Marsh (left) and John Hixson in pensive mood on the shore, 1890s.

90. The Swanage lifeboat *Herbert Sturmey* on the slipway at Peveril Point in 1924. The boat was in service from 1918 to 1928 and was the last to be powered by oar and sail. Swanage lifeboat station was established in 1875.

91. David Hibbs, lifeboatman, 1906. Hibbs served in the *William Erle* from 1893 to 1914. Note the cork life-jacket.

92. (*Above*) The Royal Victoria Hotel, The Parade, about 1900. The central part was built as a private house in 1721, the wings were added later and it became a hotel in 1823. It owes its name to a visit by Princess Victoria in 1833. In the 1960s part of the building was a popular pub called The Pit. The building has survived – it was converted to a pub, club and flats in 1978 – but its elegance and the gardens have long since gone.

93. (*Left*) Gathering seaweed on the beach, for use as fertiliser, 1895

94. (*Left*) Searching for stranded fish at low tide, 1895. As well as making fish torpid, and therefore easier to catch, the bitterly cold winter of 1895 caused widespread unemployment in Purbeck. Six weeks of hard frost brought work to a standstill, and the men in this photograph were all unemployed.

95. Bicycle races on the sands, 1895.

96. Wartime defences, summer 1945. The war is over, but some of the anti-invasion defences remain. Mines, barbed wire and further scaffolding defences had been removed the previous year. These defences were never needed, but Swanage was bombed many times from the air, causing much damage and loss of life.

97. Summer crowds on the beach, 1950s. Swanage saw a revival as a resort after the war and before foreign beach holidays became affordable and popular.

98. The wreck of the *Olive Branch*, Peveril Point, 1895. The vessel came to grief during a spell of freezing weather, when salt spray froze on the rigging.

99. The wreck of the *Netto*, February 1900. This Norwegian schooner, carrying salt from Cadiz to the Shetland Islands, was driven onto the Peveril ledges in a violent south easterly gale. Visibility was bad and the captain thought he was rounding the Isle of Wight. The crew of five, plus the ship's cat, were rescued by breeches-buoy.

100. Swanage Station, 1886. The branch line from Wareham to Swanage opened in May 1885, nearly 40 years after it was first proposed. The first engine, a works engine for use by the contractor, was hauled from Wareham by road, before the line was completed. This meant negotiating the steep hill up to Kingston as there was no adequate road through the valley from Corfe Castle to Swanage at the time. The town grew rapidly in the wake of the railway's opening, becoming an established resort. The picture shows a Beattie well tank locomotive, and station staff.

101. Swanage Station, 1966. The locomotive is a British Railways standard class 4, 2-6-0, built in 1953. The last steam engine ran the following year and the line closed in 1972, despite an attempt by a preservation society to buy the line. Since then the Swanage Railway Society have overcome a succession of obstacles and successfully reinstated the line as far as Norden.

102. Panton's Brewery, about 1886. The brewery and manager's house, centre, occupied the site of what is now the health centre. The buildings were demolished after 1893 and the station goods yard was later extended over the site. The station can be seen on the right. The brook was later channelled and the shops on the south side of Station Road were built over it. This picture, taken from what is now Station Road, shows how rapidly this part of the town changed after the arrival of the railway.

103. (*Right*) Station Road, looking east, about 1895. Brook Farm and Dairy, centre, were on the site of the present Barclay's Bank, on the corner of Mermond Place, and were demolished in 1914. Beyond the cart, the Mowlem Institute can be seen. It was built in 1863 by John Mowlem, founder of the engineering firm which still bears his name, as a reading room 'for the benefit and mutual improvement of the working classes.' It was demolished in 1965 and replaced by The Mowlem Theatre.

104. Farm buildings behind Brook Farm, about 1889. It is hard to imagine such a scene in the middle of Swanage now. This is now the site of an amusement park.

105. High Street, looking west, about 1915. This was the main focus of the town until the arrival of the railway created a new area for development. Visible are two buildings incorporating bits of old London brought to Swanage by stone 'baron' George Burt. In the centre of the picture is Purbeck House, built in 1875 for George Burt and now a hotel. The gazebo includes bits and pieces salvaged from the original Billingsgate fish market. On the right, the frontage of the Town Hall, built in 1882, incorporates the 17th century facade of the Mercers' Hall.

106. Church Hill, about 1900. The tower of St Mary's Church is all that survives of the medieval building, originally built as a chapel-of-ease to St Nicholas's Church, Worth Matravers. The priest would commute between the two along the Priest's Way. The cottages at the bottom of the hill were bombed in the war and the rectory garden now occupies the site. The town pump on the right was replaced by a large cross erected in memory of Sir Reginald Francis Palgrave who died in 1909 and had been Clerk to the House of Commons.

107. Mr and Mrs Selby, 1898. Mrs Selby was the local midwife and also 'laid out' bodies for burial.

108. Thomas Bennett's garage, Lynden Hall, Ulwell Road, 1905. Bennett also had premises in Institute Road, as a carriage proprietor.

109. Stone quarries at Cowleaze, about 1910. This area was once riddled with small quarries for extracting building stone and the so-called 'Purbeck marble'. Though not a true marble, it can be polished, and was used for decorative work in churches and for memorials. The workings were mostly underground as the stone occurs in relatively narrow seams which dip to the north. Swanage took over from Corfe Castle as the centre of the Purbeck stone industry after the destruction of the castle in 1646, and quarrying was the main industry of the town until the end of the 19th century. Much of the stone was exported to London, particularly after the Great Fire of 1666, for building stone and paving. These old workings have now disappeared under housing and Hoburne Caravan Park.

110. Swanage quarrymen, about 1920. On the left is 'Crusty' Norman, third from left is Alf Norman.

111. A quarry at Cowleaze, about 1910. In the foreground is the capstan with the chain for hauling up small wagons loaded with stone from underground. The capstan was turned by a donkey harnessed to the 'spack', a wooden bar which fitted through the hole. The stone was worked in the 'quarr huts' seen behind the men. On the left is Fred Meader.

112. Harry Chinchen (left) and Walter Brown working by candlelight in an underground quarry, about 1920. Underground quarrying was in decline by this time; the last quarry closed in 1939.

113. Quarrymen's demonstration, Court Hill, 1898. The quarrymen marched from Langton Matravers to the stone depot at the bottom of Court Hill, in protest at the jailing of George Lander, who had defied an injunction by opening a quarry on the grounds that an ancient charter gave anyone the right to open a quarry. The load of stone the men took with them was not accepted at the depot, so it was thrown in the sea.

114. The Great Globe, Durlston Head, about 1905. Swanage benefactor George Burt installed the Globe, one of the most remarkable sights in the Swanage area, in his public park at Durlston Castle in 1887. It was made in his London works of Portland Stone, in 15 sections, and weighed 40 tons. It shows the oceans and continents, and the British Empire at a time when Britain was at the height of its imperial power. Behind the globe are stone panels inscribed with geographical and astronomical information, all part of the Victorian tradition of education for the people.

# *Langton Matravers*

115. The High Street, Langton Matravers, about 1895. The row of 17th century cottages on the left once stood opposite the King's Arms, but all but the furthest of these have since been demolished and replaced by more modern housing. Beyond the last one, the tall building was the village bakery, latterly White's, from 1866 until it closed in 2001. Langton Matravers is strung out along a street nearly a mile long, and it was already like this in Saxon times, for Langton means 'long settlement' in Old English. Matravers originates from the Maltravers family who owned it in the 14th century.

116. A stone wagon on Steps Hill, Langton Matravers, about 1895. Stone quarrying was the main industry in Langton, and the grinding and squeaking of wagons taking the stone to the 'bankers' at Swanage was part of village life. The men of Purbeck were skilled in the art of moving heavy pieces of stone. Before the days of motor lorries and hydraulic hoists, stone had to be manhandled and moved by horsepower. Descending with a loaded wagon required the use of iron skids that could be dropped under the wheels if the load 'took charge.' There was no seat for the carter – in this case Alfie Masters – so he had to walk!

117. Durnford School, Langton Matravers, 1930s. In the early 20th century there were six schools in Langton. One of these was the Durnford Preparatory School for Boys, established by Thomas Pellatt in 1893 in Durnford House. The school closed in 1934 and during the war the buildings were used by scientists working at the radar station at Worth Matravers. The buildings were demolished in 1952 and rebuilt in a similar style but without the magnificent gazebo.

118. Dancing Ledge, 1930s. The cliffs of Purbeck are pitted with old quarry workings, leaving caverns and ledges where Portland stone between Durlston Head and St Aldhelm's Head was blasted and chiselled away. The name Dancing Ledge has two alternative origins: one, because it was as big as a ballroom floor, the other, because incoming waves appear to dance over it. Thomas Pellatt, headmaster of Durnford School from 1893, owned the land which included the old quarry and the schoolboys would start their day with a walk to the Ledge and a swim, naked, in the sea. Pellat had the 'swimming pool' seen here excavated for the boys to use when the sea was too rough.

119. Langton Matravers Orchestra, 1893. The orchestra was set up by Mrs Frances Serrell of Durnford House, who was keen to encourage the cultural life of the village and provided instruments and tuition. The leader was Samuel Thompson, in the centre, with bow. The orchestra, pictured in the grounds of Leeson House, kept going after her death in 1888.

# Acton

120. (*Above*) Ethel Hobbs of Acton, about 1925. Acton is a small hamlet of former quarry workers west of Langton Matravers. Here Ethel Hobbs drives cattle along the untarred road from Kingston to Langton west of the turning to Worth, against a backdrop of quarries and spoil tips, with Swanage Bay in the distance.

121. (*Opposite page top*) Maurice Hobbs, Ethel's brother, outside his cow shed which still stands on the north side of Acton Gate (the turning to Acton), about 1925.

122. (*Opposite page bottom*) Brief encounter at Acton Gate, about 1925. Nurse Pushman, who lived in Worth Matravers, was the local midwife, and her working life was spent travelling around the region delivering generations of Purbeck babies. The man with the bicycle may be Ben Lander. He had poor eyesight which led to the occasional collision.

# *Worth Matravers*

123. Worth Matravers from the east, about 1900. The village is situated on the limestone plateau, with cottages built out of the local stone. Quarrying was the main industry in recent times, and London Row, the terrace on the left of the picture, is a reminder that quarrymen and masons often had to seek work in the capital. The Church of St Nicholas, built around 1100, was the mother church of St Mary's, Swanage, in medieval times. This view is now obscured by the trees which have since matured.

124. St Aldhelm's Head Quarry, 1968. This is the only quarry in Purbeck now producing Portland limestone. Purbeck limestone, for building and paving, is also quarried in the Worth area, as is 'Purbeck marble.' This is not a true marble, but a limestone largely made of freshwater shells. In medieval times it was exported all over England for use in columns, fonts, and effigies in cathedrals and churches. Building stone was used for medieval churches and manor houses, and later for general house building. All underground quarrying was outlawed in 1963, on safety grounds. Here we see quarry owner and sculptor Treleven 'Trev' Haysom.

125. Worth Matravers, about 1910. Worth is a picture-postcard village with its duck pond and cottages roofed in Purbeck stone slates. Before the wall beside the spring-fed pond was built, it was a muddy farmyard pond used by cattle from Worth Manor Farm, and in the early days of motoring the occasional car ended up in it. In the late 19th century Rose Cottage, beyond the pond, was the home of cobbler James Lowe, who made 'straights,' boots which could be worn on either foot.

126. RAF Worth Matravers, near Renscombe Farm, 1960s. The station opened in 1942 as part of the 'Gee Chain' navigation system for aircraft on bombing raids over Germany. It occupied the site of the Telecommunications Research Establishment, built in 1940 to develop the new technology of radar, which enabled incoming enemy aircraft to be detected and intercepted before reaching the coast. This establishment moved to Malvern in 1942 to avoid being bombed. The RAF station closed in the 1960s when the Gee system was superseded.

# Kingston

127. St James's Church, Kingston, 1890s. This magnificent Victorian church, known as the 'cathedral' of Purbeck, was completed in 1880. It was commissioned by the owner of the Encombe Estate, the third Earl of Eldon, as the family's private chapel. It was built lavishly of local stone and marble, giving a welcome boost to Purbeck quarrymen and masons, and it dwarfs the small hamlet of Kingston. An earlier St James's Church was provided for the village by the first Earl in 1833 on the road to Langton Matravers, and is now a house.

128. (*Below left*) The street, Kingston, 1950s. Kingston was built as an estate village in the late 18th century, by the enlightened and philanthropic William Morton Pitt of Encombe, who also set up a short-lived factory making sailcloth, cordage and sacking. The village has hardly changed since.

129. (*Below right*) Scoles Farm House, 1910. Scoles, in the valley between Kingston and Corfe Common, is a fine 17th century house incorporating much older elements. Although standing alone, it may well be the only survivor of a medieval hamlet, which is how many of the farms in the valley between the chalk ridge and the limestone plateau originated.

# *Corfe Castle*

130. West Street and the Castle, 1890. The castle, Purbeck's most famous landmark, commands the main gap in the Purbeck ridge. It was fortified in late Saxon times, but the ruins date mainly to the early middle ages when it was a royal castle and Purbeck was a royal deer forest. It was captured by parliamentary forces in 1646, during the Civil War, and subsequently deliberately destroyed. The village grew up to serve the castle, and for centuries it was the centre of the Purbeck stone trade. 'Purbeck marble' and building stone were brought here from the limestone hills to the south to be worked in workshops on West Street, after which it was taken to Ower Quay on Poole Harbour for export. With the demise of the castle the centre of the stone trade shifted to Swanage.

131. The 13th century outer castle gate, 1890s. The notice reads 'Notice is hereby given that All Persons Removing or throwing any Stones From the Castle Walls Will be PROSECUTED,' and shows how attitudes to the ruins had changed from earlier centuries, when they were plundered for building work in and around the village! The notice was put up by the then owners, the Bankes family, who had owned Corfe Castle and large estates in Purbeck since 1635. Ralph Bankes, who died in 1981, bequeathed all this land to the National Trust.

132. (*Above*) The annual ceremony of the 'Ancient Order of Purbeck Marblers and Stone Cutters,' 1950. The long tradition of stone working in Purbeck is commemorated every Shrove Tuesday, when members kick a football from Corfe Castle to Ower Quay where they sprinkle a pound of pepper over it, representing payment to the tenant of Ower Farm for keeping the lane to the quay open for the traffic of marble. The ceremony dates back many centuries to the time when Corfe Castle was the centre of the Purbeck stone trade. Marblers nearest the camera are, left to right, George Bower, Alfie Meader, Bob Bower, Ralph Meader, Nelson Burt and Arthur Hancock.

133. (*Opposite page top*) West Street, Corfe Castle, about 1930. West Street was the main thoroughfare of the town until the late 18th century, when East Street became part of the turnpike road to the south. West Street became a backwater and now ends at Corfe Common, once crossed by various tracks from quarries and hamlets. In this view, looking south, Woadden's grocery can be seen on the right.

134. (*Opposite page bottom*) Corfe Castle and Vineyard Cottage, about 1930. The name of this 17th century cob and thatch cottage may indicate a former vineyard. Nearby are traces of three medieval fishponds.

135. Mitchell's forge, Corfe Castle, about 1900. The forge, on the northern approach to the Square, was a favourite local meeting place. The blacksmith had a reputation as a man of the world, having met many travellers passing through or visiting the castle. The building is still a shop and the forge survives.

136. West Mill, Corfe Castle, 1890s. A mill was first recorded on this site, west of the castle, in the 13th century. These buildings became redundant and were converted into cottages at the end of the 18th century, only to be demolished in about 1920.

137. Lifting the rails of the Swanage branch near Corfe Castle, 1972. The ten mile branch line from Wareham to Swanage survived Dr Beeching's axe but by the end of the 1960s its future looked grim. The line closed in January 1972, and, even though a preservation group had formed and attempted to buy the line, British Rail quickly removed the track from Swanage to Furzebrook. From here the last three miles to Wareham were left for the carriage of clay from the ECC Ball Clays works, and for BP's projected gathering station there. Over the years a group of determined enthusiasts have reinstated the line and the stations as far as Norden, north of Corfe Castle, with the intention of ultimately re-opening the entire line to passenger traffic.

138. A Drummond M7 tank locomotive built in 1905 steams out of Corfe Castle heading for Harman's Cross and Swanage, 1998. This engine worked the branch up to the early 1960s when it was withdrawn and sold to an American transport museum. It was brought back to Purbeck in 1987 and now, fully restored, is a familiar sight on the Swanage Railway.

# *Church Knowle*

139. The street, Church Knowle, 1930s. At this time the village was self-contained, with a shop, post office, school, 'reading room,' (all of which have now closed), and a church and pub. The reading room, seen here on the right of the road, was provided in 1887 by Rev Owen Luttrell Mansel to commemorate Queen Victoria's golden jubilee. Reading rooms were a Victorian innovation which gave working men the opportunity to read and spend their leisure time constructively. The building still stands, though it is disused.

140. (*Opposite page top*) The New Inn, Church Knowle, 1930s. The inn was originally part of a small farm, and when this photograph was taken the thatched building was still the dairy, producing butter and cheese. The licensee was Bob Savage, one of several members of the Savage family to run it over many years. Mr Savage was also a taxi driver, and his car can be seen on the left. The dairy became a bar, with its own entrance, in about 1957.

141. (*Opposite page bottom*) Drinkers outside the New Inn, about 1900. The man on the right is Arthur Hobbs, later landlord of the Greyhound Inn, Corfe Castle, and the man on the far left is possibly James Horlock of Puddle Mill Farm.

THE
NEW
INN

142. Gerald Savage of the New Inn transporting milk churns at Blackmanston Farm, about 1905. He may have been delivering the milk to the milk depot at Corfe Castle railway station or to his family's dairy at the New Inn.

143. Gerald Savage with hay cart at Cats'l Corner, west of Church Knowle, 1930s. Mr Savage married Church Knowle schoolmistress Victoria Burden, and they took over Church Farm from her parents. Their son Victor is second from the right. The horse was Bonny.

144. Charlie Green of Whiteway Farm, at Wareham Market in the 1970s. Charlie was a well known local character who started a motorised livestock transport business in the 1920s when he was at East Creech Farm. Charlie provided many services to the local community, including pig slaughtering and contract harvesting.

145. Fox digging at Whiteway Farm, about 1940. To country people foxes were a pest, particularly when it came to poultry, and controlling them was seen as a necessity. Terriers were sent in to the den to kill the fox, and often had to be dug out. The boys are Stan Green, left, and Tom Christopher. Dorothy Green (later Savage) is on the left and Mrs Elsie Best on the right.

146. Pupils and staff of Church Knowle School, 1929. The school was established in 1855 and closed in 1938. These children were identified by Mrs Queenie Stockley and Mr Victor Savage in 2001. The names of many old Purbeck families are represented here, and are listed left to right.

Front row: Ken Collins, Ern Simpson, Gordie Hyde, Sid Drinkwater, Arthur Collins, Charlie Drinkwater, Willie Burt, Leslie Green, Jim Green. Second row: Cissy Bugler, Iris Simpson, Daphne Savage, Cicily Savage, Betty Usher, Mabel Green, Doris Hooper, Edith Saunders, Phyllis Simpson, Daisy Green. Third row: Dougy Green, Donald Abbott, Victor Savage, Miss Amy Bradford, Mrs Smart (headmistress), Miss Matthew, Bob Bugler, Archie Hyde, Victor Mears. Fourth row: Rose Collins, Dorothy Bartlett, Phyllis Marshallsay, Violet Collins, Cecily Usher, Nellie Stockley, Nancy Collins, Ada Mullett, Eve Mullett. Back row: Jack Abbott, Eric Hyde, Frank Green, Cycil Webber, Claude Abbott, Fred Bartlett, Fred Simpson, Ted Savage.

147. Land Army girls at Church Farm, Church Knowle, about 1941. During the war there was an acute shortage of labour as men were drafted into the services, leaving women to fill posts which were traditionally men's. Farming was crucially important, and the Women's Land Army was established to provide a pool of volunteer labour at key times in the farming calendar, such as hay-making and harvest. Here we see Wendy Holbrook (later Pushman) leading a horse-drawn hay sweep.

# *Kimmeridge*

148. The oil well at Kimmeridge Bay under construction, 1959. The BP Exploration Company struck oil at a depth of 2,800 feet in 1959, and installed 'nodding donkey' pumps, which are still operating. Continued explorations eventually led to the discovery in 1974 of the reserves which are now tapped from Wytch Farm and other sites on the shores of Poole Harbour. Oil is also found in a narrow band of oil shale exposed in the cliffs at Kimmeridge. The shale was mined commercially in the 19th century, and was also burned locally as a fuel, giving off a foul-smelling smoke.

149. Clavell Tower, Kimmeridge, originally built as a folly by the owner of nearby Smedmore House in 1831. This photograph shows the tower when it was being used a coastguard's look-out towards the end of the nineteenth century. The flagpole's stays were attached to old cannons dating back to the Napoleonic wars.

# *Tyneham*

150. Post Office Row, Tyneham, about 1900. This was the main street of the village, with the post office and village shop, the second house from the left. At the end of the street is St Mary's Church, dating from the 13th and 18th centuries. Tyneham is now in ruins, for in December 1943 the valley and surrounding areas were requisitioned by the army for tank training in preparation for the invasion of occupied France. The inhabitants of Tyneham and of several other hamlets and farms were evacuated; this was to be a temporary measure, but after the war the army retained the area.

151. The wedding of Lilian Bond of Tyneham House and her cousin Herbert Ivo Bond of Creech Grange at St Mary's Church, Tyneham, 18th June 1914. The service was conducted by the Bishop of Salisbury. Lilian Bond wrote the classic memoir of life in the valley as she had known it, *Tyneham, a Lost Heritage.*

152. Tyneham House, about 1890. This house, once one of the finest manor houses in Dorset, was built by Henry Williams in 1583, and incorporated a 14th century hall as its west wing. The Bond family bought the house and the estate in 1683 and remained the owners until the War Office compensated them for what it had commandeered in 1943. This view shows the east and north fronts, from the drive.

153. Tyneham House after demolition in 1968. The house was taken over by the RAF in 1941, for use as support facilities for the radar station set up at Brandy Bay. After the war it was abandoned, thieves stole lead from the roof, and bits of the interior and exterior were taken away to other country houses. The decision by the War Office and the Ministry of Works to demolish the main part in 1968 was a scandal at the time. It contrasts with the care and expense subsequently put into tending the ruins of the village, maintaining the church and restoring the schoolroom after Tyneham was officially opened to the public at weekends in the 1970s.

154. School children's outing to Tyneham, probably from Creech, the other Bond estate on the other side of the hill, about 1900.

155. Worbarrow Bay, 1920s. Until 1943 there was a small community at Worbarrow Bay, seen here from Worbarrow Tout. The Miller family of fishermen and smugglers lived here for generations, in Sea Cottage at the head of the beach and in other cottages. Sheepleaze, the large house on the left, was built as a holiday home around 1920. The house on the right had been a coastguard station until 1911, when its associated row of cottages was bought and demolished by the Tyneham squire, William Bond, to prevent them being sold as holiday houses.

156. Edwardian trippers at Worbarrow Bay, with Sea Cottage and fishing boats behind. In the 18th century Worbarrow Bay was a favoured spot for smugglers, who on one occasion held a fair on the beach to sell off their contraband. Lookouts armed with pistols were ready to engage the excise men, who were usually heavily outnumbered. On another occasion some excise men pursued a smuggler to the west end of the beach where, encountering a sheer rock face, the fugitive took to the sea, where he was stoned to death by his pursuers.

157. Operators of the Brandy Bay radar station, early 1940s. In addition to elaborate anti-aircraft defences, the RAF opened a number of radar stations along the Purbeck coast during the war. One of these was above Brandy Bay east of Tyneham, from where incoming enemy aircraft were tracked, in conjunction with similar stations on St Aldhelm's Head and on Portland, both visible in line of sight. The information was communicated to the command centre at Middle Wallop in Wiltshire. This photograph of the WAAFs, taken at Worbarrow Bay, captures the spirit of wartime camaraderie. Note the coastal defences in the background.

# *East Lulworth*

158. Lulworth Castle on fire, 1929. Lulworth Castle was built by Thomas Howard in about 1610 in military style but with no military function, and the present owners, the Weld family, bought the estate in 1641. The castle was gutted by fire on 29th August 1929, and reduced to a shell. The cause of the fire was never established. Soldiers from the gunnery school together with some girl guides camping in the grounds assisted castle staff in rescuing furniture and paintings. Restoration of the outer shell, and the building of a new roof, began in the 1970s and the castle opened as a 'roofed ruin' in 1998.

159. The post office, East Lulworth, 1903. East Lulworth is a picturesque village, with thatched cottages, post office (now closed), and pub. The missing element is the church, some distance away near the castle. In the late 18th century Edward Weld decided that the village was too close to his home, so a whole street, leading to St Andrew's Church, was 'removed', leaving the church alone on the edge of a field.

160. Arish Mell, 1930s. The western ends of the two ridges of Purbeck hills terminate at Worbarrow Tout, the headland in the distance, and Arish Mell, a small cove breaching the chalk ridge. Before 1939 Arish Mell was a popular beauty spot, and the spectacle of cattle wandering on the beach was common. It was closed on the outbreak of war and incorporated into the expanded Lulworth and Tyneham tank ranges in 1943. A coast path opened in the 1970s, but in the meantime (1959) a huge discharge pipe had been built to the beach from the nuclear power station at Winfrith, making it out of bounds to the public.

161. The Lulworth Tank Gunnery Ranges, late 1920s. In 1916 Bindon Hill, between Lulworth Cove and Arish Mell, and land to the north was used for testing the army's new secret weapon, the tank. So secret was it that whenever tanks moved along public roads, outriders went ahead making sure that nobody would be able to see them. In 1923, against fierce local and national opposition, the War Office requisitioned this area, described at the time as 'the most exquisitely beautiful stretch of the Wessex coast.' The picture, looking east, shows Medium Tanks firing on the move at a target range on Bindon Hill.

# *West Lulworth*

162. A camp of Dorset volunteers above Lulworth Cove, 1865. Many of these volunteer regiments were established during the Napoleonic Wars to defend the nation against invasion while the regular army was campaigning abroad. They formed the basis of what is today called the territorial army.

163. Lulworth Cove, 1901. Lulworth Cove became a popular attraction in Victorian times, due mainly to the summer paddle steamer services. Regular services between Bournemouth and Weymouth, with stops at Swanage and Lulworth, began in 1874 and continued until the 1960s. Here we see the *Victoria*, launched at Weymouth in 1884. She was requisitioned for war service in both World Wars, and was finally scrapped in 1953. Most of the 'paddlers' have gone, but the splendidly restored *Waverley* regularly visits Dorset and keeps the tradition alive.